Returning to Afghanistan

CRABTREE
PUBLISHING COMPANY
WWW.CRABTREEBOOKS.COM

Linda Barghoorn

Author: Linda Barghoorn

Editors: Sarah Eason, Harriet McGregor, and Janine Deschenes

Proofreader and indexer: Wendy Scavuzzo

Editorial director: Kathy Middleton

Design: Paul Myerscough and Jessica Moon

Cover design: Samara Parent

Photo research: Rachel Blount

Production coordinator and
Prepress technician: Ken Wright

Print coordinator: Katherine Berti

Consultants: Hawa Sabriye and HaEun Kim, Centre for Refugee Studies, York University

Produced for Crabtree Publishing Company by Calcium Creative

Publisher's Note: The story presented in this book is a fictional account based on extensive research of real-life accounts by refugees, with the aim of reflecting the true experience of refugee children and their families.

Photo Credits:
t=Top, c=Center, b=Bottom, l= Left, r=Right

Inside: Afghanistan Needs You: p. 28b; Flickr: Ninara: p. 25t; ResoluteSupportMedia: p. 22b; Shutterstock: Anahit: p. 13; AndriyA: p. 9b; Artisticco: p. 12b; Awsome Design Studio: p. 3; Brothers Good: p. 6t; Derek Brumby: p. 5b; Evellean: p. 19b; Faber14: p. 27b; Gil C: p. 5c; Wandel Guides: p. 16c; Isovector: p. 18br; Iana Kauri:p. 25b; Helga Khorimarko: pp. 18bl, 20t; Michal Knitl: p. 14t; LineTale: p. 16; Maximum Exposure PR: p. 9t; Mspoint: p. 28t; MSSA: pp. 4t, 11b; Bruno Pagnanelli: p. 6b; Parose: p. 12t; Lizette Potgieter: p. 24; Viktorija Reuta: p. 20bl; Ricochet64: p. 21t; Sudowoodo: p. 29t; VectorOK: p. 14; What's My Name: pp. 4l, 7b; UNHCR: © UNHCR/Roger Arnold: pp. 14-15b, 16t, 17; © UNHCR/N. Farhad: p. 12c; © UNHCR/Sara Farid: p. 4; © UNHCR/ Jim Huylebroek: p. 7t; © UNHCR/Sebastian Rich: pp. 10-11b, 18c, 19t, 20c; © UNHCR/Jason Tanner: pp. 9c, 15t; Wikimedia Commons: Kanishka Afshari/FCO/DFID: p. 11t; Masoud Akbari: p. 23; DoD photo by Chief Hospital Corpsman Josh Ives, U.S. Navy: p. 26b; Kandara: p. 22t; Spc. Jeanita Pisachubbe: pp. 10b, 20br; NATO Training Mission-Afghanistan/ Communications Specialist 1st Class Elizabeth Thompson: p. 27; USAID Afghanistan: p. 26r.

Cover: © UNHCR/Roger Arnold.

Library and Archives Canada Cataloguing in Publication

Barghoorn, Linda, author
    Returning to Afghanistan / Linda Barghoorn.

(Leaving my homeland : after the journey)
Includes index.
Issued in print and electronic formats.
ISBN 978-0-7787-4985-1 (hardcover).--
ISBN 978-0-7787-4991-2 (softcover).--ISBN 978-1-4271-2127-1 (HTML)

    1. Refugees--Afghanistan--Juvenile literature. 2. Refugee children--Afghanistan--Juvenile literature. 3. Return migration--Afghanistan--Juvenile literature. 4. Repatriation--Afghanistan--Juvenile literature. 5. Afghan War, 2001- --Juvenile literature. 6. Refugees--Afghanistan--Social conditions--Juvenile literature. 7. Refugees--Social conditions--Juvenile literature. 8. Afghanistan--Social conditions--Juvenile literature. I. Title.

HV640.5.A28B37 2018   j305.9'0691409581   C2018-903019-4
    C2018-903020-8

Library of Congress Cataloging-in-Publication Data

Names: Barghoorn, Linda, author.
Title: Returning to Afghanistan / Linda Barghoorn.
Description: New York, New York : Crabtree Publishing, 2018. |
  Series: Leaving my homeland: after the journey | Includes index.
Identifiers: LCCN 2018029858 (print) | LCCN 2018031391 (ebook) |
  ISBN 9781427121271 (Electronic) |
  ISBN 9780778749851 (hardcover) |
  ISBN 9780778749912 (pbk.)
Subjects: LCSH: Refugees--Afghanistan--Juvenile literature. | Refugees--Pakistan--Juvenile literature. | Refugee children--Afghanistan--Juvenile literature. | Refugee children--Pakistan--Juvenile literature. | Afghan War, 2001---Refugees--Juvenile literature.
Classification: LCC HV640.5.A28 (ebook) |
  LCC HV640.5.A28 B37 2018 (print) | DDC 958.104/71 [B] --dc23
LC record available at https://lccn.loc.gov/2018029858

Crabtree Publishing Company
www.crabtreebooks.com   1-800-387-7650

Printed in the U.S.A./092018/CG20180719

Published in Canada
Crabtree Publishing
616 Welland Ave.
St. Catharines, Ontario
L2M 5V6

Published in the United States
Crabtree Publishing
PMB 59051
350 Fifth Avenue, 59th Floor
New York, New York 10118

Published in the United Kingdom
Crabtree Publishing
Maritime House
Basin Road North, Hove
BN41 1WR

Published in Australia
Crabtree Publishing
3 Charles Street
Coburg North
VIC, 3058

What Is in This Book?

Sonita's Story: Pakistan to Afghanistan

Hello! My name is Sonita. I live in Afghanistan. It is my homeland. But I did not even set foot here until I was nine years old. I learned all about Afghanistan from stories my mother told me. Now we live in Afghanistan, and I have at last met my grandparents, aunts, uncles, and cousins!

*I grew up in a **refugee** camp called Kot Chandna, in Pakistan. I lived there with my family. The camp was far from perfect. But at least we were safe from the fighting in Afghanistan.*

UN Rights of the Child

A child's family has the **responsibility** to help ensure their **rights** are protected and to help them learn to exercise their rights. Think about these rights as you read this book.

Some students go to school in Kot Chandna refugee camp. This is not the case in all refugee camps.

UZBEKISTAN

TURKMENISTAN

TAJIKISTAN

IRAN

Afghanistan

Kot
Chandna

Afghanistan is
located in the
center of Asia.

PAKISTAN

ARABIAN SEA

Afghanistan's flag

Pakistan's flag

But, over time, life became difficult for us in Pakistan. Pakistan's government took away many of our rights. It made plans to **deport** us. My parents said we could no longer stay there. We prepared to return to Afghanistan.

I had been a refugee my whole life, so I did not know what life in Afghanistan would be like. I knew that it was still not a safe place. But it would be safer for us than Pakistan. I was nervous and excited. I just wanted to go to school, make friends, and live happily with my family.

My Homeland, Afghanistan

Afghanistan has great mountains and dry deserts. It has a wonderful **culture**, and history. It is a center for art and music. It has ancient cities such as Kabul. But this beautiful country has seen conflict, or fighting, for many years.

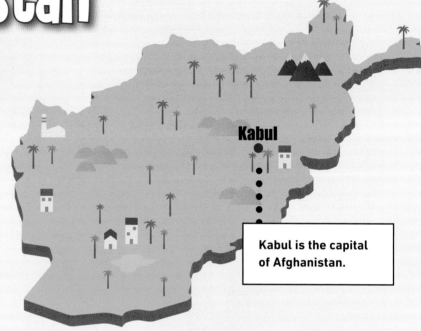

Kabul

Kabul is the capital of Afghanistan.

Kabul is in a valley in the Hindu Kush mountain range.

From 1996, a terrorist group called the **Taliban** was in control of Afghanistan. It enforced very strict laws. Afghanistan became home to other **extremist** groups, such as Al-Qaeda. On September 11, 2001, Al-Qaeda flew airplanes into the Twin Towers in New York City, and into the Pentagon, in Washington, D.C. The United States then led a war against Afghanistan.

Many people in Afghanistan are **internally displaced persons (IDPs)**, because of fighting between the Taliban, ISIL, and the Afghan government's army.

The war ended in 2014, but there is still fighting in the country. The Taliban and **Islamic State in Iraq and the Levant (ISIL)** fight the Afghanistan government. This has destroyed much of Afghanistan. Millions of people fled their homes. Many refugees tried to find safety in neighboring countries, such as Pakistan and Iran. But these countries forced the refugees to return to Afghanistan. Many other countries, including the United States and Canada, have also deported refugees. Deporting refugees is against the **UN Refugee Convention**, which states that refugees should not be sent back to a country where they face danger.

Today, there are often **terror attacks** in Afghanistan. The Afghan government fights **militants** for control of the country. Thousands of people are injured and killed each year. The government is not able to provide enough food, shelter, medical care, and education for its people. The **United Nations (UN)** calls the situation there a **humanitarian crisis**.

Story in Numbers

In 2017, the UN estimated that one-third of Afghanistan's population of

27 million

people needed aid.

Sonita's Story: Returning Home

Policemen carefully guard Afghanistan's borders, or areas that divide countries. They are guarded to control who enters Pakistan.

I was only eight when we left Kot Chandna. My baba (father) and older brother Izat had both lost their jobs. Then the police arrested Baba. He disappeared for days. The police questioned him about a nearby terror attack. I knew my baba would never be involved in such a terrible crime. After Baba came home, the police threatened him every day. We knew we had to leave.

*My mora (mother) packed our few precious belongings. The **United Nations High Commissioner for Refugees (UNHCR)** gave us some money to help us start new lives in Afghanistan. It was more money than we had ever seen.*

I was so sad to leave my friends, Farah and Samia. I had grown up with them. We promised to try to find each other one day.

Afghanistan

Kabul

The journey from Kot Chandna to Kabul is about 310 miles (500 km).

Kot Chandna

Pakistan

During 2016, more than
600,000
refugees returned to
Afghanistan from Pakistan.

Some IDPs live in temporary homes in Kabul. It is hard to survive there.

We traveled by bus to the border between Pakistan and Afghanistan. We waited there for hours. Finally, we were allowed to cross into Afghanistan.

When we reached Kabul, it was not what I had expected. The roads and buildings were ruined. I worried: Had we made the wrong choice in returning home? Would we ever be safe here?

A New Life

Many refugees who have returned to Afghanistan knew how dangerous it would be. But with refugee camps becoming unsafe, many chose to accept money from the UNHCR to return to Afghanistan.

Back in Afghanistan, the refugees found conflict and **poverty**. The president promised to give refugees land in the countryside so they could build new homes. But most refugees believed there would be better jobs and education in the city of Kabul. Land in Kabul is expensive and hard to find, so refugees have struggled to build a life there.

In addition to giving an allowance of $400 per refugee, the UNHCR pays for shelter, such as this house, for returning families.

Most refugees have also received little help from the government. Instead, family and friends have had to help them find shelter, jobs, and schools. Refugees who have lived for years—or their whole life—outside of Afghanistan may have to learn the language and culture of their homeland.

Some Afghan refugee children who have lost their parents live in orphanages in Afghanistan. This US soldier is visiting an orphanage school.

You have the right to special protection and help if you are a refugee.

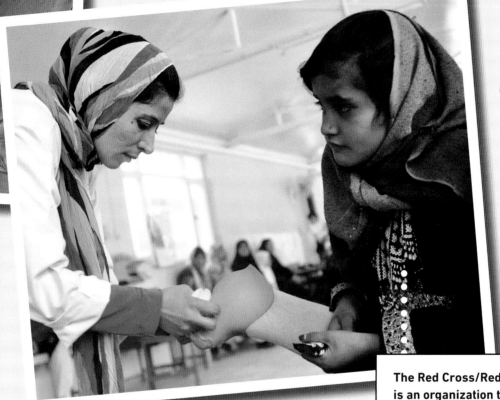

The Red Cross/Red Crescent is an organization that helps people in times of disaster. This Red Cross/Red Crescent doctor is treating a refugee.

Many international organizations work in Afghanistan. The Afghan Red Cross/Red Crescent helps refugees and IDPs find family members. **UNICEF** and Save the Children sponsor education centers. Local job training programs help adults find work. Other organizations help rebuild schools, hospitals, and roads.

Sonita's Story: Arriving in Kabul

The bus took us to a busy station in downtown Kabul. There were crowds of people, cars, and carts. There were still bullet holes from the war in some of the buildings. Baba collected our packages and found a taxi for us. We made our way to the address Mora's cousin had sent her.

We arrived at an old building, and climbed two flights of stairs to an apartment. A small, thin man opened the door. He shouted when he saw us. Then a tiny woman rushed to the door. It was my anaa (grandmother)! She cried and hugged us so tightly. Soon everyone was crying and hugging.

Refugees can bring only what they can carry or load onto a bus when they return to Afghanistan.

Story in Numbers

The number of people living in Kabul has more than tripled in size since 2001, from

1.5 to 4.6 million

people. Returning refugees and people fleeing conflict in the Afghan countryside have flooded into the city.

The apartment was crowded and noisy. Majeed, my mother's cousin, has taken care of Anaa since Mora's brother, our Uncle Noor, left for Europe. Two other cousins and their families live there, too. While we were there, Mora asked me to send a text to Uncle Noor using Uncle Majeed's phone.

We stayed with Uncle Majeed for a week. Then Baba found us a place to live outside Kabul. Baba has also applied for a piece of land from the government.

Mora is happy to be near anaa again. But my parents are shocked at what has happened to Afghanistan. There is so much poverty, sadness, and damage from the war. Many people have nowhere to live. Some mosques provide them with a place to sleep at night, but often we find people begging in the streets for food.

Dear Uncle Noor,
Baba, Mora, Izat, Hala, and I arrived in Kabul on Monday. We went to Uncle Majeed's apartment, where I met my Anaa for the first time. We will take good care of her now that we are back in Afghanistan. I hope one day she can come to live with us when we build our house here. What is Germany like?
Your loving niece,
Sonita

A New Home

Hundreds of thousands of refugees have returned to Kabul. The city has become overcrowded. It struggles to provide basic services such as proper health care, clean water, and electricity. Although some of the city has been rebuilt, most returning refugees and IDPs cannot afford apartments there. Instead, they live in houses that they have built themselves on the hillside areas around Kabul.

Chaman-e-Babrak is one of these areas. There, many people live in mud houses. The area is dirty, and human waste sometimes runs through the streets. Some neighborhoods have no power for up to 15 hours a day. Women and girls walk to wells to collect water for cooking, drinking, and washing.

Because it has become so overcrowded, places to live in Kabul are expensive.

The Afghan government has relied on foreign governments and organizations, such as the UNHCR, to help rebuild the country. Yet most Afghan people still live in terrible poverty.

Cities, towns, and villages across Afghanistan have been almost destroyed by the conflict. The government faces a huge task to rebuild the country.

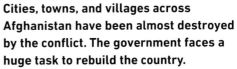

Well-paid jobs are hard to find in Afghanistan. Many people can find only a few hours of work, and this work is often poorly paid. It is difficult for parents to earn enough money to provide for their families. Often, they take their children out of school so that they can also work to earn money.

UN Rights of the Child

You have the right to food, clothing, and a safe place to live.

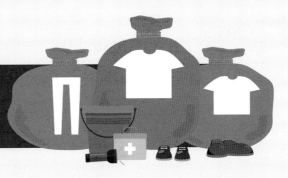

Sonita's Story: My New Home

Soon after we arrived in Kabul, my Baba looked for the home where he had lived with my Mora and Izat before the war. But it was no longer there. Strangers lived in the house that had been built in its place. So, we have rented a house. It is in a crowded neighborhood on the very edge of Kabul.

Our rent is $33 a month, and much of our money goes toward it. Mora worries that all our UNHCR money will be spent on rent before we can build our own home. Baba hopes the government will give us land to build on soon.

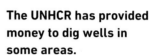

The UNHCR has provided money to dig wells in some areas.

These homes are on the hillsides surrounding Kabul.

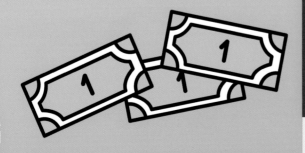

Story in Numbers

More than
$60 billion
in aid has been donated to help rebuild Kabul. But most people there still live in poverty.

Baba has bought a used cell phone. He calls many people looking for extra work and asking for help with our land application. One day, he let me use it to contact my friend Farah in Pakistan. I sent a text to her mother's cell phone.

Baba and Izat wake at 4 a.m. to go to work. After school, I help my mora with chores such as cooking, cleaning, and washing. We walk to the well each day to get water. I cannot go on my own because my parents worry I might be attacked. Sometimes I think life in Kabul is even more difficult than it was in Kot Chandna.

Refugees often cook with just a single pot over an open fire outside their home.

Farah, are you still in Kot Chandna?
I am living in a neighborhood called Jamal Mina. It is outside Kabul. We will stay here only until Baba can buy some land and build a better home. I hope it is in a place that is not so crowded and dirty. I miss you. Please tell me if you move somewhere new. I hope we will see each other again soon.
Sonita

17

A New School

The government wants children from returning families to go to school in Afghanistan. But many of the country's schools have been destroyed. Only some have been rebuilt. Classrooms are crowded. If there are no school buildings, classes are held outdoors.

During the Taliban's rule, millions of children did not go to school. Their parents did not think they would be safe there. After the war, many went back to school. But now that refugees have returned to Afghanistan, there are not enough schools for all the students. Many communities do not have enough trained teachers or school supplies such as books and paper.

Because of strict religious beliefs, many families will not allow their daughters to be educated by men. If there are no female teachers, girls may be taken out of school.

UN Rights of the Child

You have the right to a good quality education and should be encouraged to achieve the highest level of education you can.

These boys are enjoying a few minutes of play at this UNHCR-funded school near Kabul.

Many Afghanis still think that it is less important to educate girls than it is to educate boys. Under the strict rule of the Taliban, girls could not go to school at all. Today, girls are returning to classrooms. But some have been attacked by people who do not want them to go to school.

Some organizations build schools and provide teachers in Afghanistan. Many have programs to help children catch up on the education they have missed. More than 3.5 million Afghan girls are now in school. But still, about four in ten Afghan children do not attend school.

Sonita's Story: My New School

Every day, Mora takes my little sister Hala and me to school. In the morning, Mora waves goodbye as we enter the school gate. In the afternoon, she waits outside to take us home. A girl was attacked last year on her walk to school. Now, none of the mothers allow their daughters to walk alone to school.

In the winter, I wear a coat and gloves in class. There is no heating. When it is too cold, our classes are canceled. Sometimes, there are not enough textbooks for all of us. We have to share.

Many schools in Afghanistan are built with money from outside aid organizations, such as the Norwegian Refugee Council.

Many international organizations provide children in Afghanistan with important school supplies.

Dear Samia,
How are you? Are you still living in the camp?
Today was a good day for us. Books, pencils,
pens, and paper were delivered to our school.
It was like we all had a birthday! I'm so
excited. Thank you, UNICEF!!
Love, Sonita

Without charities, I would not have school supplies.

I am in my fifth year of primary school in Kabul. I work hard to improve my reading and writing in Dari, our local language. I really love learning more about our national culture in class. Many of the girls in my class have also grown up as refugees outside Afghanistan. My best friend Tara grew up in a refugee camp in Iran.

At the end of next year, I will have to pass an exam to go to middle school. My teacher from Kot Chandna, Madame Aqeela, believed that girls should have the same education as boys. I want to make her proud of me. I hope I can go to university one day, too.

Story in Numbers

In 2001, while the Taliban ruled Afghanistan, fewer than

1 million

children were in school.
They were almost all boys.
Today,

9 million

children attend school and

3.5 million

of them are girls.

Everything Changes

Afghanistan was once a peaceful and beautiful country. It will be many years before its people can return to the lives they once enjoyed. While some are hopeful for the future, others are not so sure. Thousands of Afghans continue to leave their homeland every year.

Some parts of life in Afghanistan are slowly returning to the way they were before the conflict. The Taliban banned, or did not allow, entertainment. This ban has been lifted. Families can share a weekend picnic in the park. They can drink a glass of tea in a café, or visit the Kabul Zoo. Tradition and family play an important role in the life of every Afghan.

Some neighborhoods in Kabul have been rebuilt. They have modern buildings and smooth paved roads.

People in Afghanistan can once again enjoy kite-flying, soccer, and music. Kite-flying is one of the country's most popular activities, for both children and adults.

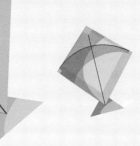

UN Rights of the Child

Children have the right to follow and practice their own culture, language, and religion.

Mosques, like this, are places where people can gather to pray. Religious traditions are important in Afghanistan.

In the past, women had many of the same rights as men. They had an education, jobs, and freedom to make their own choices. The Taliban took away many of these rights. Today's Afghan women are fighting for their rights. Women once again have the right to vote.

People still fear that the Taliban could return. But they also look to the future. They hope for a stronger Afghanistan. In the cities, some people have well-paid jobs. They can afford to go to the shopping malls, cinemas, and restaurants. But many Afghans still remain too poor to afford these activities.

Sonita's Story: My New Way of Life

Since returning to Kabul, we have had to say goodbye again to some of our family and friends. They are too scared to stay in Afghanistan, so have decided to leave. But Baba and Mora say our family's future is here. They do not want to leave our anaa again, and will not go.

Baba is now training to become a construction (building) manager. He smiles when he talks about rebuilding our country. With so much work to be done in Afghanistan, Baba hopes he will make good money. He has bought a cell phone. He is very proud of it, too! Sometimes he even lets me call Farah and Samia on it.

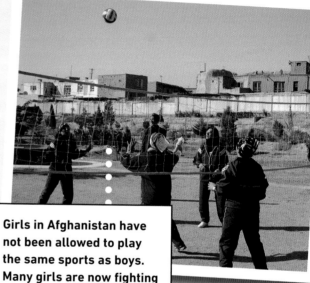

Girls in Afghanistan have not been allowed to play the same sports as boys. Many girls are now fighting to change this.

Farah,
Today, I watched Zan TV. It is Afghanistan's first television station run by women. These women are fighting for the rights of girls and women in Afghanistan. I want to follow in their footsteps to help create a better future for Afghan girls.
Sonita x

Story in Numbers

Today, more than half the population of Afghanistan is under the age of 25. They use the Internet and technology to connect to the world. They will make decisions about Afghanistan's future.

People sell brightly colored cloth for women's clothing at a market in Kabul.

Mora sells crafts in a women's market to earn some extra money. She makes beautiful shawls. She takes them to the market each Wednesday afternoon. Sometimes, I go with her after school. I help set up her table and I talk to the customers.

On the weekends, our family enjoys walks and picnics at the Kabul Zoo. Other countries have donated many of the zoo animals. Hala and I love to learn about them. Sometimes, Izat takes us to the park, where we fly kites. We see whose kite is the strongest and whose can fly the highest!

Sonita's Story: Looking to the Future

Last week, Baba finally got news from the government. We will receive a small plot of land to build our house. It is the best news we have had since returning to Kabul! Baba draws plans and pictures of what it will look like. Baba says, we can finally plan for a real future in Afghanistan.

At school, we are learning about Afghan women who take big risks. They speak out for women and girls in our country so that all our voices will be heard.

This woman is about to vote in an election. In elections, people vote to decide who will lead the country.

Women now work in journalism in Afghanistan. Journalists report the news and share their ideas and stories with people.

I try to be a strong voice for girls at school and at home. Some of my friends are worried. They do not know if they will be able to continue their studies. They worry their parents will make them get married and raise a family before they are ready to.

I believe girls should be allowed to go to school, just like boys, and even go to university. My parents support me. But they do wonder how we will pay for university fees. But I will find a way—I am determined to! Just as we are rebuilding our country, I am building a good future for myself!

UN Rights of the Child

You have the right to live in a safe environment with hopes and dreams for the future.

Afghan women wear the uniform of the Afghan National Army. These women are preparing for a ceremony at the end of their training.

Do Not Forget Our Stories!

Refugees who have returned to Afghanistan work hard to rebuild their lives and communities. They have proven just how strong they are. They have overcome many challenges in a difficult and very dangerous place.

Young Afghans educate others about how to work toward peace in Afghanistan. They want to improve the rights of all people there. A social media campaign called #AfghanistanNeedsYou encourages Afghanistan's young people to help build a stronger, better Afghanistan. The campaign organizers spread awareness by painting murals, or wall paintings, in different parts of the country.

These young people are painting a mural for the Afghanistan Needs You campaign. They hope to encourage people to stay in Afghanistan and to volunteer to help improve their communities.

Some Afghan refugees have started new lives in other countries around the world. There, they are important parts of their new communities. They work hard to stay in touch with their homeland, but also welcome a new way of life far from home. In their new countries, they celebrate their Afghan culture and beliefs, while also learning about their new country's culture and beliefs.

Refugee children around the world face many risks. They flee conflict, **discrimination**, and violence. When they return to their homeland, they often face uncertain and even dangerous lives. Although these stories may not make news headlines every day, many of these people still need our help. The first step is to learn about and remember their stories.

Discussion Prompts

1. Why are many Afghan refugees living outside their homeland worried about returning home?
2. Why do so many Afghan children not complete their education?
3. What positive changes have happened in Afghanistan since the Taliban lost control?

Glossary

culture The shared beliefs, values, traditions, arts, and ways of life of a group of people

deport Remove from a country

discrimination Unfair treatment of someone because of their race, religion, ethnic group, or other identifiers

extremist Having a strong belief in something; often political

humanitarian crisis An event that brings harm to the health, safety, and well-being of a large group of people

internally displaced persons (IDPs) People who are forced from their homes during a conflict, but remain in their country

Islamic State in Iraq and the Levant Also called ISIL, ISIS, or Islamic State; a group of extremist Muslims who believe that people who do not share their beliefs are enemies

militants People who use strong and sometimes violent means to achieve their goals

poverty The state of being very poor and having few belongings

refugee A person who flees from his or her own country to another due to unsafe conditions

responsibility The duty to deal with something

rights Privileges and freedoms protected by law

Taliban A terrorist group of militants that follows an extremely strict interpretation of Islam

terror attacks Attacks by groups that use violence to achieve their goals

UN Refugee Convention An international agreement about how refugees should be treated; nations cannot deport refugees

UNICEF United Nations Children's Fund; a global organization that defends and protects the rights of children

United Nations (UN) An international organization made up of 193 countries that promotes global peace

United Nations High Commissioner for Refugees (UNHCR) A program run by the United Nations that protects and supports refugees everywhere

Learning More

Books

Bjorklund, Ruth. *Afghanistan* (Enchantment of the World). Children's Press, 2018.

Ellis, Deborah. *Kids of Kabul*. Groundwood Books, 2012.

Mattern, Joanne. *Afghanistan* (Exploring World Cultures). Cavendish Square, 2017.

Websites

http://teacher.scholastic.com/scholasticnews/indepth/old_reports/afghanistan/kid_q_a.htm
Experience everyday life in Afghanistan through the eyes of children.

www.trustineducation.org/why-afghanistan/life-in-the-villages
Read all about daily life for people living in villages in Afghanistan.

www.unicef.org/rightsite/files/uncrcchilldfriendlylanguage.pdf
Explore the United Nations Convention on the Rights of the Child.

Film

The Breadwinner
A film about a young girl living in Kabul, Afghanistan, who must dress as a boy to support her family. Suitable for ages eight and up.

Index

About the Author

Linda Barghoorn studied languages in university because she wanted to travel the world. She has visited 60 countries, taking photographs and writing stories about the people and cultures of our planet. At home, she volunteers at a local agency that provides newcomers and their families with clothing and community support.